Stand in the Gap for Your Children

by
Norvel Hayes
and
Zona Hayes Cornelison

Harrison House
Tulsa, Oklahoma

Unless otherwise indicated,
all Scripture quotations are taken from
the *King James Version* of the Bible.

14th Printing

Stand in the Gap for Your Children
ISBN: 978-089274-886-0
(formerly ISBN 0-89274-257-7)
Copyright © 1991 by Norvel Hayes and
    Zona Hayes Cornelison
P. O. Box 1379
Cleveland, Tennessee 37311

Published by Harrison House, Inc.
P. O. Box 35035
Tulsa, Oklahoma 74153

Printed in the United States of America.

Contents

Introduction

As you read the following pages, you are going to see how much the Devil hates your children.

Those readers familiar with my ministry, who have listened to my tapes or read my books, have heard me speak of my daughter, Zona. Also, you have heard me tell about so many of her teenage friends dying.

You may have wondered if all of the stories I told were true, or if I exaggerated to make a point. In the following pages, you will read Zona's first-hand account of what happened.

The Devil is exposed in the following chapters. You will discover exactly how the Devil entices young people to the point where he can kill them. I hope you will see that you must begin to "stand in the gap" for your child and rescue him, or her, from the Devil, death, and hell.

Norvel Hayes
Cleveland, Tennessee

Part 1
by Norvel Hayes

1

Stand in the Gap
for Your Children

*I sought for a man among them, that should make
up the hedge, and stand in the gap before me.*

Ezekiel 22:30

Standing in the gap is serious business. The eyes of
the Lord go back and forth, looking for someone who will
stand in the gap for someone else.

When someone is away from God, there is a gap
between that person and God. He is not able to fill that gap
and come to God because his faith is too weak. Someone
else is needed who is willing to pray and stand in faith in
the gap between that person and God. By praying and
standing in faith, the Christian builds a bridge for the weak
person to come to God.

This can be done for groups of people or even for entire
cities, but in this book I want to teach you how to stand
in the gap for your children.

How I Stood in the Gap
For my Daughter

I learned how to stand in the gap by praying for my
daughter Zona.

When Zona was nine years old, my world fell apart.
Even though I thought I had it together really strong, I was
just playing church. From that day forward I raised my

daughter alone. Zona would wake up at night, wringing her hands, because her home had broken up.

I prayed every night that God would visit me. That was all I had to do, and every night the Spirit of the Lord visited me. I would wake up and reach for my Bible. Then God would come into my room. He would literally shake me in my bed, sometimes for two or three hours. I've had the Lord to shake me all night until eleven o'clock in the morning. I would lie there with the Spirit of God moving up and down my body, tears gushing out my eyes, as He burned all the chaff out of my life.

I prayed that God would touch my mind and lead me to people who could teach me things. I just kept following the Lord, and He just kept opening doors before me.

One time when Nicky Cruz and I were working the streets in London, England, the Lord knocked me down and began to talk to me. It nearly scared me to death! Have you ever had Jesus just knock you down? It was like walking into a white cloud. I began to weep.

The first words He said to me were, "Go get the Bible. You can't live your life over again." When I got the Bible, it was like picking up an electric wire.

When Jesus knocked me down, He talked to me for three or four minutes. Then His presence started to leave the room, and I began to come back into the natural realm. He told me years ago exactly what I would be doing right now. All that He told me has come to pass. Glory be to God!

When Zona was sixteen, she started dating a boy in our church. His name was Bobby. Both of them had already received the baptism of the Holy Spirit. I never had any problems with this young man.

When Zona was seventeen, I allowed her to stay out until 11:30 P.M. if she and Bobby went to get something to eat after church. Bobby took her to church regularly and always brought her in on time, never questioning me. He was just as nice and kind as he could be.

One day they told me that Bobby was going into the service. He had already graduated from high school and gone to college. They had decided that after Zona went to two years of college and Bobby got out of the service, they would get married. I said, "Fine."

When Zona graduated from high school, she enrolled at a Full Gospel college in town.

One morning as I was getting ready to leave town, the Spirit of the Lord spoke to me and said, "I don't want them to get married. Beware! Watch that boy."

You could have knocked me over with a feather, but I knew it was the Spirit of God. The Holy Spirit knows everything and can reveal the truth to us. To be successful, all we have to do is get the mind of the Lord.

I kept what He had told me secret for a while until I heard that Zona and Bobby were thinking about getting married earlier than they had planned. They said they missed each other too much.

One night I went over to the college and called Zona down to the lobby. I told her how the Lord had spoken to me. I said, "It's not God's will for you to marry Bobby, at least not now. Don't ask me to explain anything, but I'm just telling you what the Lord told me."

Zona said, "It may not be God's perfect will for me to marry Bobby, but I think I'm going to anyway."

"Get your fighting clothes on, then, because you're going to need them," I told her.

When the Spirit of God tells you not to do something, you had better not do it! I don't care who you are or where you come from, if God says, "No!" then He means, *No!* You may never know why He says it; He doesn't have to tell you why. Sometimes He may show you; sometimes He may not. But if God said, "No," then don't do it!

In spite of what I told Zona, she and Bobby started planning the wedding. Bobby's mother wanted them to get married. She liked Zona and thought she was a sweet girl, so she promoted the marriage.

Bobby was coming home every two or three weeks and Zona was living in the college dormitory. She wasn't supposed to leave without my signing out for her, but one Saturday night Bobby's mother signed Zona out and took her home.

They found two preachers who would marry them. I went to both pastors' homes and talked to them. I said, "It's not God's will for you to marry my daughter to this boy. I just thought I would come and tell you so that when they get a divorce, you can say I had told you so. God said, 'No!' "

Then I said, "I'm not going to cooperate with the wedding. I'm not going to give Zona away. Jesus said, 'No!' so I just can't do it. I like the boy myself, but God said that Zona shouldn't marry him."

I told both pastors that the decision to perform the ceremony was between them and God.

The plans continued, and when Zona asked if I would give her away, I said, "No. God told me He doesn't have anything to do with it, so I won't have anything to do with it. I love you, honey. Because I love you so much, I'll walk you down the aisle, but that's as far as I'll go."

On the day of the wedding, I stood out in front of the church as *Here Comes The Bride* started playing. Zona was standing there in her wedding gown.

"Zona, honey, this is your last chance. Jesus said, 'Don't do it!' My car is full of gas. If you'll get in the car,

I'll go up in front of that full auditorium and say, 'There isn't going to be a wedding tonight!' "

She started laughing and said, "Daddy, you just love me so much, you don't want to give me away."

"No, that's not it. Jesus said, 'Don't do it!' "

"Daddy, everything is going to be all right."

"No, it won't, Zona. God said it wouldn't; and if God says something, that's the way it is. I don't know what the future holds, but *He* does."

Our walk down the aisle was a long one for me. When I got down front, I just turned around and sat down. I went to the reception and acted like I was enjoying it, but I wasn't. I was just putting up a front. Why? Because the Spirit of God in me had said, *No!*

One Sunday morning about three or four weeks later, Zona came to church alone. Bobby had never missed church in the two years before that. After that, he missed some night services; then another Sunday morning service, then another.

By that time Zona had begun to see the light, to see what was happening to her.

When she got home from church, she would find Bobby dressed up. He would say, "Come on. I'm going to take you out to dinner."

But Zona would say, "No, you're not. If you can't go to church with me on Sunday morning, then I won't go with you to the restaurant after church."

A year later, they were divorced.

At age nine, Zona was surprised at her mother. As an adult, she was surprised at her husband. Finally, she decided to quit going to church and start going her own way. She got her own apartment and got involved in drugs. She started taking "speed." For two years she "dropped pills'' and didn't darken the door of a church. I had been praying for her, so I just kept on praying!

When she came to the house, she barely spoke to me. Sometimes I wouldn't see her for a month or two, even though we were living in the same city. I had to stop her credit cards because she kept running up charge accounts. She just did what she wanted to.

I began to pray even more. Sometimes the Devil would make me feel like a failure and a phony. He would say, "You're a good one! You've lost everything. You don't have a home anymore. Here you are sitting alone, with your daughter living in the same city."

For nearly two months I felt like all the blood had been drained from my body. Though I felt like a failure, I kept going on.

"Oh, no, Satan," I said. "I remember how Jesus visited me in His mighty power." Saying this began to melt and burn the junk out of me.

I said, "No, you don't, Satan. Jesus has never let me down, and I'm not going to let Him down! I can't help it if all my relatives go to hell — I'm not going to hell!"

I just kept going on. I went to the Florida beaches to pass out tracts. I gave my testimony across the country. I went everywhere I could to work with young people.

One day as Zona strolled through the house, she said, "Where are you going next weekend?"

"I don't know," I said. "Maybe New York or maybe California."

"I bet it makes you feel funny, Daddy, going around the country trying to win other kids when you can't win your own."

The Lord told me to tell Zona like it is, so one day I sat her down and said, "Zona, honey, listen real close and believe me. I'm not going to hell. If I did what you wanted me to do, I would go to hell. But I'm not on the same path you are, and I won't be on it, either! And *you* aren't going to stay on it, Zona, because I'm going to pray you out of it!"

So I just kept praying and praying and praying. I kept crying out to God. I wondered, *When will my daughter get out of darkness? How long is it going to be?*

I prayed so long and so hard that I didn't even know how anymore. After you pray for something six months, you begin to wonder if God even hears you. After a year, you begin to believe He doesn't hear. After two years and things get even worse, you *know* He doesn't hear!

2
God Dealt With Me
To Love Zona, More

After holding a meeting in San Antonio, Texas, for ten days, I went to Houston to catch a plane for Chattanooga. Fifteen minutes before I was to leave, the Spirit of God came on me suddenly. (That's what makes the difference: the Spirit of God!) He told me to call Rev. J.R. Goodwin. Rev. and Mrs. Goodwin were pastors of the First Assembly of God Church in Pasadena, Texas, just outside Houston. I hadn't seen the Goodwins in five years.

When I called, Rev. Goodwin asked me to come see him, so I went. The missionary who had taken me from San Antonio to Houston was there. We hadn't been in the Goodwins' living room more than five minutes when the Spirit of God came on me. The missionary began to speak in tongues and interpret. After the second message, I began to weep. The Lord began to speak to me. He told me to go to Tulsa, Oklahoma. He said, "I will show you two things after you get there."

As I was on my way to Tulsa, He said, "The things you love the most on Earth will not come to pass as long as you continue living and praying under your present conditions. There is something more you need to know."

"What is it, Jesus?"

"Your daughter is in so much darkness and her faith is so weak that she will never be able to get out of that darkness. Her faith is too weak for me to bring My power to her to break that darkness, but your faith has been wavering and it won't work."

"Where has my faith been wavering, Jesus?"

"You have been wondering why I don't hurry up and do it," He said. "I have to be pleased with your faith before I can do what you are asking. Stand in the gap for your daughter with an unwavering faith, and I will come to her. I will manifest Myself to her."

When you pray for something for two years without getting it, you will become nervous if you aren't grounded in God's Word. God wants you to trust Him with patience. Anything outside of patience is doubt. If you don't have the peace of God about what you are asking God for, you are in doubt and it won't work.

"Besides that," the Lord said, "you haven't been loving her right. When Zona comes in at one or two o'clock, you haven't been reaching out to her like I reached out to you when you were in sin.

"I didn't come against you when you were in sin. I want you to reach out to her when she comes in. I want you to tell her how much you love her."

I was the one who had to change. I began to watch my mouth and stand with an unwavering faith.

When Zona would come in at one o'clock, I would say, "Come here, honey." I would have her sit beside me, then I would tell her how much I loved her.

As I watched Zona backing out of the driveway at night, I knew she was going to the dance hall. Her girl friends told me that Zona would completely take over the dance floor and do the "Funky Chicken." (That's a screwy name for a teenage dance.) No matter what her friends told me, I refused to let my faith waver.

Every time Zona would put on her mini skirt and walk out the door, I would go to the picture window. As I looked out, I would stand on God's Word, quoting His promises. I got my spirit grounded in God's Word.

As I watched her drive off, I would tell the Devil, "I won't let you have her. You can't have her. You're not going to kill her." I would say, "Thank You, Jesus, for bringing Zona back into the Kingdom of God." I just kept on thanking and praising God that Zona was coming back into the family of God.

After several months of that, Zona began to date Bobby again. I thought, *Oh, no! This can't be real!*

When God had told me that Bobby and Zona shouldn't get married, I didn't know why. But even though they loved the Lord, He knew what was going to happen. When Bobby started dropping out of church, Zona backslid, too, because she loved him so much. Now here I was, facing the same crazy mountain again: that goofed-up boy!

I told Zona, "God told me that you shouldn't marry Bobby, but you did it anyway. I know how old you are, but I'm not going to put up with it again."

She kept seeing Bobby, so I told her he couldn't come into my house. I said, "I'm not going to let the Devil just walk in and take you off!"

I stood my ground!

My relatives told me I was making a mistake.

"I don't care!" I said. "I'm not making a mistake until God says I am. When God tells me differently, I'll let Bobby come in."

For months when Bobby came to get Zona, he would stop in the driveway and she would meet him there. I refused to give in. I stood my ground!

Before long, Zona began to talk about marrying Bobby again. I couldn't believe it! "You don't really mean that, Zona. You aren't that dumb!"

"My girl friends told me I couldn't get him back, but he wants to get married."

In spite of all this, I just kept standing steadfast in faith and claiming her complete deliverance. I praised God that Zona was back in church and completely delivered. I had to see her deliverance and restoration in my spirit and confess it with my mouth.

I just kept on praying and praying and praying!

One day as I was walking back and forth across my living room praying, I felt like laying my hands on Zona's bed. As I did, I said, "God, this house belongs to You. Everything I have belongs to You. I'm not trying to tell You how to do anything. Just do what You want to do. As she lays in this bed tonight, Jesus, work her over. Shake her up."

About four o'clock the following morning, Zona woke up screaming. When I went to her room, I found her standing by the door, trembling. She had opened her eyes to see her angel sitting on the floor, looking at her. He was sitting there with his legs crossed, staring straight at her.

"Daddy," she said, "I got so afraid that I couldn't scream. When he saw that I was afraid, he got up and walked out of my room. I know I wasn't dreaming. It was real! I jumped out of my bed and watched him walk down the hall, then he turned and walked right through the wall! He was wearing clothes, but he just walked through the wall!"

She was scared half to death. I told her what had happened to me and that he was her angel. She started screaming and crying out to God.

Despite everything, Zona and Bobby got married again. They moved to Alabama, but God wouldn't let her get away from that angel. When she slept, her angel stared at her. She got so frightened that she wrote me a letter, begging

19

me to pray. She said she couldn't get away from that angel and that he was about to scare her to death.

About that time Kenneth Hagin came to town for a seminar. He came a few days early to stay at my house and pray. One night around midnight he and I were sitting in my den. We began to pray together. We had prayed in tongues for almost an hour when Brother Hagin received the interpretation. I began to shake.

The Lord told me through this interpretation that He had dealt with Bobby, but that Bobby had not listened to the wooing of His Spirit. He said He was fed up with Bobby's rebellion.

God gets tired of continuous rebellion. You can only push God so far in anything. When you step over that last step, you had better watch out, because destruction will be there waiting for you. Bobby was a stubborn boy and God was getting tired of his three years of rebellion.

Through Brother Hagin's interpretation, the Lord said that Bobby was about to step into a deep, dark valley. Then Brother Hagin began to weep and say, "Oh, it will be so dark, so dark."

Then God said He wanted to use me to rescue Bobby, to warn him, before he went into that dark valley. I wondered how in the world God was going to use me.

God's power was so strong that night. The Lord told us that the best way for a child of God to get an answer to prayer was for him to simply ask for what he needed. As James 4:2 says, *Ye have not, because ye ask not.* Just ask in English, then pray in the Spirit.

Brother Hagin said he had never understood the simplicity of this before. "You know," he said, "we've got hold of something I've never had before in my life."

I had been praying about this situation with Bobby for over a year with an unwavering faith. I thought I had been

20

praying for it for three years, but the first two didn't count. God told me my faith wouldn't work because it was wavering. When God says it won't work, it won't work!

Saturday night was Kenneth Hagin's last service. As Brother Hagin's son Ken was leading the singing, Bobby and Zona walked in. Ken saw a dark cloud over Bobby, whom he had never seen before.

Brother Hagin spoke, then gave the invitation. He tried to close two or three times, but God wouldn't let him. He just kept on giving the invitation. About that time Zona, weeping, stepped out alone and started walking toward the front. The power of God was all over her.

As I was standing at the side of the church, I found out how the Lord was going to use me to rescue Bobby from that dark valley. The word of the Lord came to me, saying, "Get on your face." Then He told me to have the pastor of that church agree with me for Bobby's soul. The Lord said, "He's on My territory tonight." So the pastor and I prayed together.

When we finished praying, the Lord told me to go to Bobby, put my arms around him, and tell him, "Bobby, the past is in the past and the future is in the future." The Lord told me to tell Bobby that if he didn't heed that night, a valley of darkness was going to come on him.

I went to Bobby, put my arms around him, and told him what the Lord had said. I also told him the only thing that Zona had ever wanted was a Christian home.

"Won't you give in, Bobby? Won't you give your life back to Jesus tonight?"

He agreed, then started walking to the front. When he got there, the Spirit of God came upon him. Brother Hagin put his arms around Bobby and Mrs. Hagin put her arms around Zona, who was standing there weeping before God. Mrs. Hagin gave a message in tongues and Brother Hagin gave the interpretation. I had my hands on Bobby's back.

The Spirit of God was in that place so strong! I almost had a fit! God began to melt Bobby and Zona. When Brother Hagin put his hands on Zona, she just melted onto the floor. Bobby just kept speaking in tongues. He must have spoken in tongues for forty-five minutes under the supernatural power of God. Brother Hagin said Bobby was preaching a sermon in tongues. That was a beautiful service!

Afterwards, we went to my home for fellowship. Bobby couldn't even eat because the power of God was still on him so strong.

Some time later Bobby and Zona came to a Memphis convention where I was in charge of the youth. As we were beginning, Bobby came up and asked for prayer. Richard Shakarian, Hoyt Elliot, and I took him aside. When we laid our hands on him, God knocked that 200-pound young man onto his belly. He just fell across a table.

He laid there for over three hours, unable to move. For three hours he saw little children who were naked and crying out for help. God showed him that, because Zona had a call on her life to work with children. She had a missionary call on her life and she knew it.

Some missionaries who came by said that Bobby was speaking in five languages. They gave a couple of interpretations, then left. When Bobby was finally able to get off the table, someone had to help him to his room.

From that day forward Bobby has been a changed person. You could never meet a sweeter boy! The Spirit of God came on him and cleansed him of all past sin. Let the past be the past and the future be the future.

Part 2
by Zona Hayes Cornelison

3
My Story

I really don't like to talk about the things I'm about to reveal. However, I feel the time has come to expose the Devil and his works.

First of all, I want to thank my father, Norvel Hayes, for praying for me without ever giving up and for never leaving me. I love him greatly.

My home was split apart when I was nine. At the time, I didn't understand what was happening. I only knew that my father looked different and that my mother was not around anymore.

Dad explained the situation to me the best he could for my age, and he did a real good job. He never said anything bad about my mother. So my later rebellion was not against my parents. The only reason I went through hard times in my teenage years is that I would not listen to anyone, except my dad, and sometimes not even to him. When someone told me to do something, I rebelled. Even Dad had to use a certain tone and a particular look before I would give in to his requests.

Many nights I left home with my white, bleached hair, wearing heavy eye make-up and a mini skirt, leaving my dad kneeling in prayer on the living room floor. I thought that because he was a "real religious man" I would go to heaven, too. I had once been spirit-filled, though I knew I was in a backslidden state. I thought, "God would not let Norvel Hayes' daughter go to hell. Look at the people he has gotten saved for the Lord. That would be a disgrace!"

I thought I could get by on my dad's relationship with the Lord. But I couldn't. If you believe you will get to heaven because of your mother, father, brother, sister, or grandparents, then you are mistaken; you will end up spending eternity away from God.

If you are a young person, I hope you will learn something about the Devil's traps as you read my story. Or if you are a parent, I pray that you will learn something about the importance of interceding — standing in the gap — for your children.

I Knew the Holy Ghost Was Real

I received the Holy Ghost when I was 14, even before my father received Him. We had started going to different churches — that's what my relatives called them, "different churches." As I was praying for a lady who had asked to receive the Holy Ghost, I received Him also. Dad saw me down in front of the church, praying in tongues, and said, "Oh, no! That's my daughter down there!" At that time the baptism in the Holy Spirit was new to him, too.

Some people don't feel anything when they receive the Holy Spirit, and some people do. I did, and I loved the feeling. From that experience I learned that if you pray for somebody to receive the Holy Ghost, without having Him yourself, God may give Him to you also.

When I received the Holy Spirit, I didn't even know what had happened. I just knew that I liked the feeling I experienced. It was so warm in my stomach, in my spirit. But at the age of 14, I didn't know what "spirit" was. I just knew that the baptism in the Holy Spirit was real. It meant a lot to me. And all those days later on, when I was in sin, I remembered that experience and thought about it often.

As a teenager, I didn't like people — I only acted as if I did. I did want to be accepted, however, so I became a part of a group. It wasn't a gang in the sense of Hell's

Angels, but it was made up of young people who didn't care about anyone but themselves; all they were interested in was "having a good time." I had never been a part of what might be called the "in crowd" — which is what these young people were. Because they were paying attention to me, I was pleased and thought it was a really "big deal."

I thought they were my friends, that they really liked me for myself. But later, I realized they didn't care about me the way I wanted people to care. Otherwise, they wouldn't have given me drugs.

In Search of a Mother's Love

I guess I always wanted a lot of attention because I was from a broken home. My dad gave me as much attention as he could, but still I longed for a mother's love.

All of my life I had wanted to be the center of attention, to be in the middle of everything. And I was happy-go-lucky.

I got married at an early age, even though my dad told me that the Lord had warned him that I was making a mistake. I didn't listen. Bobby and I got married anyway. When he was sent to Vietnam, people started telling me that he was probably being unfaithful to me. That is when the trouble started.

Bobby never explained to me where he was and what he was doing. People said that he would probably find a Vietnamese girl and be with her. I believed that nobody is ever faithful to anybody. Everyone I knew had been untrue to me, except for my father and a few close relatives. I felt that Bobby had slipped away from me, because I hadn't heard from him in months. I didn't understand what it meant to be on the front lines in Vietnam.

Both Christians and non-Christians told me that Bobby probably wasn't being faithful. I was barely 18 and wasn't confident enough in myself to believe that my husband (or anyone else) would ever stay true to me. Deep within my heart, I knew Bobby loved me, and I knew he would never do me wrong, but I listened to my new "friends." This is an example of why it is so important for parents to watch the company their children keep.

I went to work in a restaurant where I met people who later influenced me to start taking drugs. They really seemed to like me. I wanted their attention so badly. Their acceptance of me drew me to them and consequently pulled me away from church. They were doing all the "fun" things, like skiing at the lake on Saturday and Sunday. I couldn't go with them on Saturday because I had to work, so I went after work on Sunday. Gradually, I started doing more and more things with them. Then we started going to night clubs together.

I remember the first night I took drugs. It was the most awful feeling I had ever experienced. I felt as though I had killed somebody, because I had not been raised to do things like that.

The first time I went with the group to a club, I thought we were just going to ride around. I was nervous. I had not been brought up in that kind of life-style. I was also nervous because I wasn't old enough to drink. But my friends arranged for me to get into a club anyway.

They said, "Oh, come with us, Zona. You'll have a blast! The things we do aren't really bad!"

But they *were* bad, and at first I was miserable. By the time I got home that first night, I thought I was going to have a heart attack. I begged God not to let my father find out what I was doing, "because if he does, he will kill me!"

I was busy with my job all week, and my "friends" didn't bother me again until Friday. Then they came to the restaurant where I worked and hounded me to go out with them again.

"I can't go! I can't go!" I insisted, but they kept saying, "Yes, you can! Come on!"

I tried to find an excuse not to go. I persuaded the people I worked for to assign me to clean-up duties. It was a big job, because I worked at a restaurant where there were ice cream machines, grills, and other equipment that had to be cleaned after hours.

I wanted that cleaning job to take all night. But when I finished, the group was waiting for me.

I wound up going out with them again.

And that's how I started living a wild life in my teens. After that night, the group even helped me clean up so I could go out with them.

In the beginning, I was miserable the entire time I was with them because I was afraid someone would see me and tell my dad.

The third time I went with the group, one of the girls brought me home afterwards. I went in and lay on the floor and cried. The next morning, I didn't want to see anyone. I was so ashamed! I was from a nice family. My dad always liked people and was friendly to everyone, and I had not been brought up to party all night.

However, it became easier and easier to go out with my new friends. I liked them because they were giving me the attention I craved, and they were paying my way. Going out with them started to be fun, and I loved it. After I became comfortable with this crowd, I would head straight for the dance floor as soon as we got to a club.

I loved the attention I was receiving. My mother and Bobby had rejected me, I thought, but these people accepted me. I believed they really cared about me. When I was on the dance floor, I would "get into" the music, and all of the hurt from my mother's rejection would be blotted out. I told myself that I was having a great time.

Sin *is* fun for a season. That's how people get hooked on it, but Romans 6:23 says, ...**The wages of sin is death**.... I know this is true, because of what I saw sin do to me and my friends.

I really liked the people I was involved with. Still, what I was doing bothered me, because of my upbringing at home. It disturbed me when I began to backslide. Even when I was on drugs, I drew the line at some things. For example, I would never go to clubs on Sunday.

Descent Into Drugs

The first time my friends gave me "speed," it was one of the strongest types, called "the black widow" — the kind truck drivers take to stay awake on long hauls.

I thought it had worn off, so after three hours, I took another one. I was up all night! The next day, I went Christmas shopping and was "wired" to the sky. I loved the feeling and soon became a "speed freak."

I "did speed" every day for almost three years, and worked my way up to 12 pills a day. I worked 16 to 18 hours daily managing a restaurant in town and could not be without my constant dosages of "speed."

By then, I had become thoroughly convinced that Bobby had been untrue to me in Vietnam. Someone who knew me wrote him about the kind of wild life-style I was leading. He got an emergency leave to come home and see for himself.

The marriage disintegrated. Although Bobby assured me that he loved me and that he had been faithful to me, I couldn't believe that he wasn't untrue. Finally, he filed for divorce. And I kept right on partying.

I was a "partier," all right, but I convinced myself that I wasn't doing anything immoral — after all, I wasn't even drinking, although my friends thought I was. I just loved all the attention I was finally getting. The truth is, alcohol made me sick. One night, not long after I started going to night clubs, my friends gave me wine instead of Kool-Aid. After I had drunk several glasses of it, the room began to spin around. My friends stood around me and laughed. Their faces looked distorted to me — all large noses and big mouths.

They carried me outside to a van, and one of the girls sat with me all night while I threw up. The gang thought it was hilarious — the trick they had played on me.

So I started playing a trick of my own. When we were in a club, everybody would be "half lit" — like the club itself (it was always so dark in there it was hard to see what was going on). The group would order me screwdrivers — vodka and orange juice — and in the darkness I would pour them down onto the floor beside me. They would order me 12 to 15 drinks in one night. After a while they started calling me "little alchy" because they thought I held my liquor so well. Actually, I never drank even one of them.

There were lots of "friends" who gave me "speed."

Nearly every one of them is dead now.

I'm alive only because my dad prayed for me and stood in the gap for me. I believe many of my friends are dead because no one prayed and interceded for them.

Parents, Stand in the Gap!

If you do not stand in the gap for your children, they may die and go to hell.

You must give your children positive words and the Word of God to hear in order to build faith in them. The disgrace being brought on the family is not the most important thing you should be concerned about. What about your children dying and going to hell? If you do not want

31

their blood on your hands, pray for them and confess the Word of God over them.

Deeper Into Sin

Over the next three years, my life became progressively worse, and my drug habit progressively stronger. Yet there was always a line that I wouldn't go past. The Holy Spirit was always tugging at my heart.

There were many times when bad things could have happened to me. I might even have died. But I believe my dad's prayers prevented those terrible things from taking place.

One time, I went to a house where two or three of the girls I ran around with used to hang out, although I'd never been there before. There was plenty of food, so we got something to eat, then just sat around outside with the rest of the gang. I noticed there were several horses on the premises. When I went back inside, I saw home entertainment centers, a bedroom suite which had been taken apart, and all sorts of appliances including kitchen stoves, although I knew the house had a range because I had seen it. I thought that was strange. Out back, I had noticed there were pigs, chickens, a car, and a motorcycle.

"What's going on?" I asked. "Are we going to have an auction or something?"

My friends rushed me back outside saying, "Don't let anyone know you saw any of that stuff!"

After I got home, I realized that all of those things had probably been stolen.

The next day, we went back to the same house. We were just sitting around talking. The guy who had been stealing most of the articles found out that I knew about what he was doing. I'll never forget how scared I was. I was shaking from the inside out. My knees were knocking together, and I thought to myself, "Where's my daddy? Where's my upbringing? What am I doing here?" But outwardly, I was trying to act "cool."

All of a sudden, the guy came over and spoke to the people with me.

"If anyone knows anything that is going on around here..." he started to say. Then he slapped me across the face, knocking me right out of the chair. He looked right at me and said, "If you say anything, I'll kill you. No matter where you go, I'll find you. I'll track you until the day I die."

The Fun Didn't Last

There were ten friends in my group.

Seven of them are dead today.

It is their stories that I want to share in the next chapter.

Three others had bad things happen to them, but they aren't dead. One girl has cancer and is barely alive, another developed multiple sclerosis, and the third lost one of her legs.

Not all of my so-called friends died because they gave or sold drugs, but three-fourths of them did. They were small dealers, but they used enough drugs to cause their own deaths. I believe they died because they sold drugs to children and young people.

All of the names used in the following pages are fictitious. No hint has been given as to the identity of my friends. I'm not exposing people — I'm exposing the Devil and his methods of stealing and killing.

Young people need to be made aware of Satan's devices and traps. They must realize just how strong the influence of other people — the wrong people — can be.

Parents, love your children and stand in the gap for them! The Bible says, ... **The effectual fervent prayer of**

a righteous man availeth much (James 5:16). Don't let the Devil destroy your children!

4
Killed by the Devil

The First One to Die:

Joe was an outcast, but he wasn't a wimp, although people called him that and took advantage of him. He dealt drugs in order to be liked, and later, he began to take them himself.

We were good friends — not girlfriend and boyfriend, just good buddies. I took up for Joe all the time. In fact, all my life I have taken up for the "underdog," the person no one else likes or accepts.

Joe would sit with me at the clubs and help me cover the fact that I was pouring my drinks on the floor when no one was looking.

Night clubs are kept dark — demons like dark places — which made it easier for me to hide what I was doing. Even though my friends couldn't believe that I was downing perhaps 15 drinks in an evening, they never caught on to my trick. The owner of the club knew, of course, because every night after we had left he would have to clean up the mess I had made.

The week before Joe's death, he looked at me with tears in his eyes and said, "Zona, I wish I had never given you any 'speed'!"

"Any time you want to give me some, you just go right ahead," I told him. "I can't live without it."

Joe cried and said, "I have done this to you. I have turned you into a 'speed freak.' I'm not going to give you any more."

"What are you talking about?" I answered. "I'm not a freak. I'm having a good time. Give me some more. I need it for tomorrow." I could always talk him into giving me the drugs I wanted. Sometimes, he would even split his drug money with me. Or, if he didn't have any money, I would share with him from the small salary I made at the restaurant.

We had plans to get together the following Friday night. Joe had to work late and then help his mother, but he said he would meet me at the club. That night, I went early to the club, where there was a new band. I later learned that Joe's mother had laid out a brand new shirt and suit that he planned to wear. But when he got home that evening, he decided to lie down for a few minutes.

He tried to call the club and tell me he would be late, but the club owner would not call me to the phone. Meanwhile, I was looking all over the place for Joe. When I called his house, the line was busy.

Somehow, I couldn't have a good time that evening and Joe never showed up.

Early the next morning, when we had planned to have breakfast together, I couldn't eat because Joe was on my mind. I went home and crawled in bed to sleep for a while.

Later that morning, I was awakened by the phone ringing. I was told that that Joe had choked to death on the mucus in his throat, one of the side effects of speed. It was a miracle that the same thing hadn't happened to me. Sometimes my whole body would be pounding when it was time to go to bed, and I would repeatedly have to clear my throat.

I could not believe Joe was dead!

The funeral was just awful. His parents knew how close Joe and I had been, and they knew I was a "speed freak."

Joe had written me a little note — a gag, really — telling me that he was in jail and asking me to come bail him out. He had also written that he appreciated me because I was his best friend — the only one who had ever been loyal to him. He was going to put the note in my car. Instead, they found it on him when he died.

Joe was the first one to die . . .

The Second One to Die:

Gary drank all of the time, as well as taking "speed." One night, he was stopped by the police for driving while intoxicated. That night in the county jail, he hanged himself with his belt.

Gary was always getting citations for driving while drunk. So why did he commit suicide after this arrest? I know he did it because he thought his parents didn't care, that they didn't love him.

Gary always talked about his upbringing. There were no restrictions on him. When he was a teenager in high school, his parents didn't care what time he came in at night. They didn't care whether he got his homework done. They didn't care whether he went to school cleaned up or even whether he had anything to eat at noon. Many times, I gave him lunch money. Or I gave him my own lunch.

That's just the way it was for Gary. There were several children in the family and he was in the middle. He said that his parents just didn't have time for him. He called it being "busy." The Department of Human Services would have called it neglect.

Parents, you must not only tell your children you love them — you also need to show them kindness and love. Actions do speak louder than words, and unless you get your actions straightened out, your words alone will not mean a thing.

Gary was the second one to die . . .

The Third One to Die:

Steve went to sleep and never woke up.

We let him off at his house on our way home from the club one night, and the next morning, his parents found him dead.

I heard the announcement on the radio. The coroner couldn't find anything wrong with Steve — he had just died. My friends used to joke and say that he died partying. That would make me so angry, because even in the state I was in, I knew the truth: Steve had died and gone to hell, unless he had repented without telling anyone.

The gang kept after me to go places with them, but they called me a "stick-in-the-mud." When we went to the beach and they started that "he-died-partying" stuff, as if it were a great compliment, I would try to get them to stop.

When they were drugged up, sometimes they would say, "Let's walk on water!" And that also made me angry. Then they would call me "Little Miss Holy Girl" and laugh at me.

But even when I was in sin, I couldn't stand for them to joke about anything pertaining to God.

Steve was the third one to die . . .

The Fourth One to Die:

Mike also drank and "bootlegged" liquor. One Saturday night, he went to a nearby town to get some alcohol to bring back and sell. On the way home, he got drunk himself.

He had a wife and children, but they had gone somewhere that night. When he got home — and they owned an expensive, beautiful house — he was so drunk, he drove right through the garage wall.

Directly behind the wall of the three-car garage were the electrical outlets to the kitchen appliances. On contact with the electric current, his car exploded and burst into flames. The house, and everything around it, burned totally.

Mike's body completely disintegrated except for one gold tooth which was used to identify him.

Mike was the fourth one to die . . .

The Fifth One to Die:

Jerry was reared in a godly home, but as he grew older, he decided not to serve God.

He became mixed up with a "heavy-duty" drug crowd and began dealing dope. He sold acid (LSD), coke (cocaine), and anything else he could get his hands on. One night, he was murdered. We believe it was because he knew too much about his drug sources. In the drug world, if you know too much, your life is worth nothing. Jerry was always at the right place at the wrong time and had picked up too much information for his own good.

Jerry was the fifth one to die . . .

The Sixth One to Die:

Tim owned a well-known business, and he drank a lot. His wife was absolutely gorgeous. We used to party over at his house — really a mansion — all the time.

We thought he was great. He always provided food and everything we needed to "have a blast."

One day, he found out that his wife had been involved in an affair. He was so upset that he checked into a local motel. Arranging more than 100 pictures of her on the ceiling and walls, he lay down to die.

A diabetic, Tim purposely did not take his insulin shots. He died surrounded by his wife's pictures.

Tim was always so sweet, but he was in misery. He was a dope fiend, an alcoholic, but we never saw him lose his temper. His wife would be friendly with other guys right in front of him, but he would never show anger. I always felt so sorry for him. This time, her behavior apparently was the last straw. Tim couldn't cope, so he "checked out."

Tim was the sixth one to die . . .

The Seventh One to Die:

Jeff was a nice guy. I liked him a lot, but I never knew him extremely well.

We were at a nearby lake one night waterskiing. We always had a good time there. But when Jeff went out on the lake, he suddenly disappeared. He went under the water, skis first, and never came up. We found out that he had been pulled under by a whirlpool.

His body was never found. Ever. Talk about "blowing your mind." Some of the kids who were drunk sobered up instantly.

Jeff was the seventh one to die . . .

All This Time, My Dad Was Praying

All this time when I was out partying and "having fun," my Dad was home praying for me — standing in the gap. Deep down I knew that, one day, payment was going to come due. You may think, as I did, that partying is fun, but that kind of fun never lasts. Inside, I was miserable.

But Dad kept praying for me, and even when things in my life looked worse and not better, he didn't let up. He kept right on binding Satan from me and lifting me up before God, standing on Scriptures, and believing God for His mercy for me. If it hadn't been for Dad standing in the gap for me like that — when I was still coming home "wired" on drugs — even when he didn't have a thing to go on except God's Word, and if it hadn't been for God's mercy, I might have wound up dead like some of my friends.

If not for Dad's prayers and God's mercy, I might be in hell right now.

5

The Long Road Back

I took drugs for three and a half years, and those were three and a half years of hell for me.

For the first two and a half years, I didn't believe anybody loved me. During that time, I didn't even believe in the word *love*. Everyone, it seemed, had disappointed me, had been untrue, or had walked out on me. I hated everybody.

I started thinking more and more about my mother, and what she had done. I started blaming myself for what had happened. I never thought there was anybody who would stay with me for any period of time. I blamed it on the way I looked, because I wasn't beautiful.

I was always a hard worker — I thought if I worked real hard, maybe my father would brag on me. I always wanted Dad to be proud of me. And now I was a disgrace to him: he told me so himself.

At the beginning, even though deep down I knew Dad loved me, he would get aggravated with me. He would tell me that the Hayes family didn't do things like go to night clubs and drink and all that.

"You are disgracing me, Zona," Dad would say. "You are a disgrace to our family."

One time he even told me that he wished I was dead. He said that he would rather lose me than have to go through the agony I was causing him. In the beginning, when I was in sin, I tried my best to make that wish come true, because I didn't care whether I lived or died.

41

I thought that Dad was all I had, other than God, and I didn't really think I had God. "My mother has left," I said to myself, "and my dad will get tired of me and leave, too." I just thought that everyone would leave me — even God. That's how messed up my thinking was.

Dad was harping on me all the time about the way I was behaving, and I would say, "Dad, you're out of town all the time. How does it make you feel to know that you can go and win all those other kids to the Lord and you can't even do anything for your own child? Every time I come home, you're always helping all these other kids. You never have anything for me."

What I couldn't see was that he loved me deeply and was trying to get me to do right; he was just going about it the wrong way.

"You've Got to Start Loving Her More!"

My dad went to the home of Brother and Sister J.R. Goodwin in Pasadena, Texas, to minister in their church. From there he was to go on to Brother and Sister Kenneth E. Hagin's home in Tulsa. While traveling between Texas and Oklahoma, my dad was told by God, "The things you want the most will never come to pass unless you start loving your daughter more. When she comes in at two or three o'clock in the morning, don't start yelling at her. Tell her that you love her. Tell her that I love her. Whatever she says to you, no matter how mean or hateful she is to you, just tell her that you love her and that I love her. Then shut up."

That's exactly what Dad told me the Lord told him. And that's exactly what he started doing.

He would tell me that he was praying for me. If you've ever heard my dad speak, you know that he is very persistent about everything. He was the same way with me about coming back to God. On Sunday morning he would come in to my bedroom and say, "Zona, honey, do you want to come to church with me?"

"I'm not going to church with you," I would tell him. "Those people have talked about me and backstabbed me and I'm not going."

Later when he prayed at the table, he would say, "Thank You, Lord, for the food and everything You've done for us. And thank You that my daughter is going to church with me. I claim her soul, Lord, and I thank You that I see her raising her hands in church."

He did that all the time! It almost drove me crazy because he did it so much. Every time we sat down to eat, he did it. I told him, "Dad, I'm *not* going to church with you." And he would say, "Oh, praise the Lord that my daughter is going to church with me next Sunday. Pass the beans, Zona!"

That's how my dad is. No matter what the situation, he will not take no for an answer.

And that's how you have to be with the Devil. You can't get down. You can't get discouraged. You can't get depressed. I don't care if your child comes home drunk — love that son or daughter and thank the Lord for his or her deliverance. Then do as Dad did: bind the Devil and claim your child's soul for Jesus Christ.

As I have said, I always knew deep down that my dad loved me (especially after I came back to the Lord). Even though at the time I didn't think the love of God was shining through Dad, it really was.

After everything I've been through, I think my father is the smartest man in the world.

"Lord, Have Your Way With Her!"

Bobby still loved me when he filed for divorce. I just wouldn't have anything to do with him. Now he was back in my life and had asked me to marry him again. It was the night before I had to give him my answer.

That evening, my dad had begged me not to go out. "Just stay home," he said. "We'll pop popcorn and have a good time here. We'll be together just like a family." (I used to say that to him: "Let's do stuff, Dad, just like a family.") So that night he told me, "You don't have to go with those people, Zona."

"Daddy, I know you love me," I said. "I know you do. And I don't want to go with them."

Then he asked me, "Zona, what's it going to take to bring you back to the Lord?"

"I guess He'll have to knock me down," I answered, "because I'm not going to come back to Him. I don't trust Him. He may do me the way everybody else has done me!" I was nuts. I just wasn't thinking straight. I thought everybody was out to get Zona. But I knew my dad loved me because he stood by me. And he had changed. He wasn't yelling at me any more — he was showing me love.

After I left, Dad went into the spare bedroom and put his hands on one of the twin beds. I never slept there unless I came home real, real late and didn't want him to know what time I had come in. So he prayed, "Lord, You heard Zona. Whatever You have to do, shake her up! Have Your way with her."

Well, that night I came home about 3:00 A.M. because I had started getting numb all over. I couldn't understand it because I hadn't been drinking or anything. I had already stopped all that. I had just been out partying. So I lay down on the bed and went to sleep.

When I woke up in the middle of the morning and turned over, there was a man sitting on the floor with his legs crossed, looking right at me. I couldn't see any farther up his body than his waist, that's how big he was. The sight of this strange being scared me so bad, I started to scream,

44

but I couldn't get anything out of my throat. I didn't look up because he crossed his right leg over his left and put his right arm to the left side of his body to get up. He stood up and walked out of the room.

I pulled the quilt over my head and, peeking out from under it, looked out the door. I saw him walking down the hall. I followed him around the corner and then watched him as he walked right through the wall.

I almost fainted right there!

I thought it was a demon and that he was coming after me. I didn't know what to do. So I went to my dad's door and knocked. I tried to call out to him, but I couldn't get anything out but squeaky noises. When Dad opened the door, he asked, "What's wrong with you?"

I said, "Man! . . . Big! . . . Big, big man! I don't know . . . big, big . . . devil . . . man!"

The Lord blessed my dad by showing him that the man I had seen was my guardian angel.

That was on Thursday. On the following Saturday, Bobby and I went to the courthouse and were married again.

We moved to Alabama. But for six months, I could not get away from that vision of my angel. I kept in touch with Dad through letters, and he wrote to me about an upcoming service at Faith Memorial Church in Cleveland, Tennessee, where he would be ministering. Brother and Sister Hagin would be there. I knew I wanted to go to that service. I also knew that Bobby would be off work that weekend.

I knelt and said, "Lord, You helped me get off that 'speed' when I went 'cold turkey' for three days. I got down on my knees when I did that, too. I said to You, 'God, I don't even know how to pray to You any more, and I don't know if You'll even listen to me, but I want You to help me get off these drugs.' And You helped me."

Now I wanted God's help to get Bobby to go to that service with me. Kneeling, I prayed, "Lord, I don't know if You're even going to listen to me because of everything I've done like partying and being mean to my father — I have been hateful, really. But if You'll listen to me, would You please inspire Bobby to go with me to that service?"

It was a miracle I was asking for, because Bobby wasn't going to church either. He wasn't a mean person — he was a good person — but he just didn't go to church. We weren't doing anything wrong. We were backsliders.

To my great surprise and joy, Bobby agreed to go to the meeting. When we came into the service, Kenneth Hagin, Jr., had a vision. He saw a dark cloud over Bobby. Later he and Brother Hagin were praying during the altar call, and Dad came back to get me. I had been under conviction for six months, but I didn't return to the Lord and ask Jesus to come back into my heart until that night. I went up front, and my dad went back to get Bobby. Bobby came forward and we both dedicated our lives to the Lord. Bobby prayed for 45 minutes in tongues. And we've been serving the Lord ever since.

God Is Faithful to Restore

God is faithful. And I am so appreciative to Him, even to this day. If I let myself, when I think about it, I just weep. He restored my marriage. He brought Bobby and me back together and to Him. He has prospered us. He has blessed us with a child even after five different doctors had told me that I could never have a baby. Bobby is now in full-time ministry, and I am going to Bible school. I am also teaching full-force, speaking at a couple of meetings a month.

I am restored mentally and physically — inside and out. My mind has been healed. My body has been healed. And my mouth has been healed. (You know, your mouth has to be healed, too.) I speak no words of doubt.

That's what God has shown me — that to seek His heart, you have to pray for the mind of Christ, the heart of Christ, and the mouth of Christ.

So do parents who are praying for their children. They have to have the total nature of Christ: first the heart of Christ, then the mind of Christ. Next they have to get the mouth of Christ. When they get their words lined up with God's Word, their children will come back into the Kingdom of God as I did.

6
Don't Give Up On God!

Parents, stand in the gap for your children, and don't give up on God!

The Bible says, ...**The effectual fervent prayer of a righteous man availeth much** (James 5:16). Stand in the gap! Don't let the Devil destroy your children!

Bobby and I serve the Lord today because my dad stood in the gap and refused to give up when it looked as though nothing was happening. If anything, it looked as if my life was getting worse.

If your children have never known the Lord, the Bible says that they can come to know Him. Acts 16:31 says, **Believe on the Lord Jesus Christ, and thou shalt be saved,** *and thy house*. If your child has known the Lord but has fallen away, he or she can come back. Jesus will love your child and accept him or her, just as He did with the prodigal son. And He will restore your child's life, just as He has restored mine. Joel 2:25,26 says that God will restore the years that the locusts have eaten, the years that have been stolen from you.

Stand in the gap for your children, just as my father did for me, and don't give up!

Parents, I cannot stress too strongly that it is time for you to get down on your knees and get serious about praying for your children. It is time to stop talking to God about your problem and to begin talking to your problem about God. Otherwise, your children may never come into the Kingdom of God. Pray and confess the Word of God over your children and over whatever situation they may be in.

Remember that Satan is going to try to make it look as if God doesn't hear you and that your children won't ever turn to the Lord. But remember that Satan is a liar and a thief. The Bible says that God hears your intercession. (1 John 5:14,15.) It's His will that everyone be saved. (1 Tim. 2:1,4.) Right now, Jesus is pleading your case before the Father. (Heb. 7:25.)

The Lord is no respecter of persons (Acts 10:34): He has a miracle waiting for you just as He did for my dad and me.

Stand in the gap. Continue there in faith, no matter how bad the situation may look. Don't waver, and don't give up. Don't let the Devil have your children!

Part 3
by Norvel Hayes

7

How You Can Stand in the Gap for Your Children

In Genesis, chapters 18 and 19, we read the account of how Abraham stood in the gap for Sodom. God was going to destroy Sodom because the city had turned against Him, but Abraham interceded.

He asked God if He would destroy the righteous with the wicked. (Gen. 18:23.) Then he asked that if fifty righteous people could be found, would God spare the city. God said He would.

Abraham continued to intercede and reason with God until He agreed to spare Sodom if only ten righteous people could be found. But there weren't ten. There was only one: Abraham's nephew, Lot.

God sent two angels to Lot to tell him to leave the city because it was going to be destroyed. Lot obeyed. Genesis 19:29 tells how God remembered Abraham and spared Lot. Because Abraham stood in the gap, Lot was spared.

We see in Ezekiel 22:30 that God was looking for someone to stand in the gap for Israel. Israel had shed blood, profaned the Sabbath, lived immorally, and turned her back on God. In this case God could not find anyone who was willing to stand in the gap for Israel, so He poured out His anger upon her. (v. 31.)

It is important that you know how to stand in the gap so that you will not waste time. I had stood for two years thinking I was doing right, and God told me I had been wavering. You must not waver in your faith; wavering faith doesn't please God. To receive from God, you have to please Him with your faith.

Now faith is the substance of things hoped for, the evidence of things not seen (Heb. 11:1). Your faith brings God's power down from heaven to earth no matter what your need. The same faith that brought you salvation brings all the rest of what God has for you, no matter what it is.

Don't worry about when and how the manifestation is going to come. If you wonder *when* or try to reason *how,* you are in doubt. You are doubting God and binding His power to bring the manifestation. God doesn't need your worrying; He demands your faith.

Believe God's Word and stand on it — God will do the rest. Just be concerned about your faith and about God's promises. Leave the results to God.

Believe that you have it before you get it, before you see any results; then *wait patiently* for the manifestation.

Take control of your mouth, because it is your mouth that speaks your faith. Continually and sincerely *speak your faith by praising God for the answer* because by faith it is done. Remember, **We walk by faith, not by sight** (2 Cor. 5:7). Stand and speak your faith, no matter what you see.

Another important thing you must do is *love and not condemn.* Don't allow wrong words to slash out at your children. God doesn't like it. He wants you to reach your hands out to your children right in the midst of their sins.

Slashing out at your children, saying things like, "I taught you better than that!" shows that your spiritual pride has been hurt. I know it's spiritual pride because I've been there. I was there when Zona was running around to the dance halls.

You feel like a failure. You feel like all the blood has been drained out of your body. You sit alone in your house while the Devil points his finger at you and says, "See, it doesn't work. Why don't you stop? Why don't you go out and do what you want to do?"

When the Devil told me that, I said, "No! I'm not going to do it. I'm going to stand up for God's righteousness no matter what! My daughter is not going to hell! Satan, you're just a thief and a liar! I'm not going to let you have her. I'm going to stand in the gap for her!"

After I had reached out to Zona for six months when she was in the midst of her sin, she finally lost any desire to even go to the dance halls. "I know the people in the dance halls are phonies," she told me. "Don't you think I have sense enough to know that? Besides, it's getting so sweet in this house. I can see the difference between the way people treat me at the dance halls and the way you love me. I don't even want to go to those places anymore."

God's Obligation

Most of God's promises are conditional, and standing in the gap is conditional. *If you meet God's conditions for one who can stand in the gap, He has an obligation to perform His Word by reaching out and saving your lost loved ones.*

Let me explain what God will do when you stand in the gap. If parents will stand in the gap for their children; children, for their parents; all people, for their loved ones; God's power will rule upon the earth and honor the prayers.

If you pray right, God will honor your prayers. If you pray wrong, God won't honor them. God has standards that the human race must go by, and His number one standard is faith. Faith means you believe you have something before you get it, that you are going to trust God.

By the word of the Lord were the heavens made; and all the host of them by the breath of his mouth (Ps. 33:6).

55

The Lord looketh from heaven; he beholdeth all the sons of men. From the place of his habitation he looketh upon all the inhabitants of the earth (Ps. 33:13,14).

Our soul waiteth for the Lord: he is our help and our shield. For our heart shall rejoice in him, because we have trusted in his holy name (Ps. 33:20,21).

The angel of the Lord encampeth round about them that fear him, and delivereth them. O taste and see that the Lord is good: blessed is the man that trusteth in him (Ps. 34:7,8).

The eyes of the Lord are upon the righteous, and his ears are open unto their cry ... The righteous cry, and the Lord heareth, and delivereth them out of all their troubles (Ps. 34:15,17).

The compassion that God has upon the lonely heart, upon the heart that has been defeated in life, is amazing. When you don't know what to do, just cry out to Him for His mighty power.

The Lord hears the cry of the righteous and delivers them out of *all* their troubles. Jesus died so you could become righteous. Because you are the righteousness of God in Christ Jesus, you fit into this promise. God will hear *your* cry and deliver *you* out of *all your* troubles. It is amazing how much compassion God has for you. If you get into trouble, all you have to do is cry out to God and He will deliver you.

If you want to go your own way, God will let you; and He won't turn against you. But He will always be there waiting for you to cry out to Him so that He can perform His Word.

God watches over His Word to perform it. (Jer. 1:12.) He is obligated to do it.

Parents, all you need to do is love, believe God's Word, and stand in the gap by standing in faith on that Word. Let

God use you to reach out to your child and show His love to him. Your part is to let your light shine and praise God for producing the end result: a born-again, Christian child. God will do the rest. Let God reach out through you and perform His Word.

8

Prayers

Prayer To Stand in the Gap for Your Children

The effectual, fervent prayer of the righteous man avails much. I stand in the gap for my child, _____, who is not serving You. Jesus, I thank You that You are seated at the right hand of the Father, ever making intercession for us. Thank You that You are right now hearing my prayer and making intercession for my child. In the name of Jesus, forgive my child for getting involved with the wrong people, and for falling into Satan's snares of deception and sin. I ask You, Jesus, to convict my child of sin and at the same time reveal Your love and mercy. Cleanse my child by Your blood, Jesus, and make _____ new again.

Fill _____ with the Holy Spirit. Fill my child with joy, and reveal Your plan for his/her life. Thank You, Lord, that the plans that You have for my child are good. In Jesus' name, I confess that every one of Your good plans for my child will come to pass.

Satan, I bind you and tell you to loose my child. You let go of him/her. You let go of his/her thoughts. I break your power over my child's life, in Jesus' name. In the name of Jesus, I tell you, Satan, that you can't have my son/daughter. I take authority over you on behalf of my child, in the name of Jesus, and claim victory over you for my child.

Jesus, I thank You that my child has the desire to serve You. I thank You that You will impart to my child how important it is to have You in his/her life. Release laborers to share Jesus with _____ in just the right way. I thank You that by Your Holy Spirit, You are bringing my child into a personal, loving relationship with You.

Father, I thank You that Your Word won't return unto You void. Thank You that Your Word will accomplish what You intend for it to accomplish. Thank You for bringing my child out of the snares of the Devil and into the Kingdom of God. In Jesus' name, Amen.

Scripture References

James 5:16	Matthew 16:19
Romans 8:34	Matthew 9:38
Romans 8:27	Isaiah 55:11
Isaiah 30:18	

Prayer
for Your
Child's Protection

Father, in the name of Jesus, I pray a hedge of protection around my children. I thank You that You are a wall of fire around my children. Thank You that You have given Your angels charge over my children, to keep them in all their ways. I thank You that Your angels surround them while they are out and away from home. Thank You that You protect them from harm, accidents, and all kinds of danger.

Thank You, Lord, that You are the fortress and the refuge of my children. Thank You that Your Word is a lamp for their feet and a light for their path. Thank You that the wicked one can't touch them, and no evil will befall them.

In Jesus' name, I pray this. Amen.

Scripture References

Job 3:23   Psalm 91:2
Hosea 2:6   Psalm 119:105
Psalm 91:11   Psalm 91:10

Prayer
for the Right Friends
for Your Child

Thank You, Father, that You choose the friends You want my child to have. Lord, keep my child from the wrong influences. Provide my children with godly relationships and fun things to do that are also pleasing to You.

Father, thank You that my child walks in the way of good men and keeps the paths of the righteous. Thank You that my child will not be unequally yoked with unbelievers.

Thank You, Father, that You provide wise and godly friendships for my children. In Jesus' name, Amen.

Scripture References

Psalm 1:1   2 Corinthians 6:14
Psalm 23:3

Prayer
for Your Child's Salvation

Father, I lift my child, _____, before you. I claim his/her soul for Jesus. I thank You, Father, that You lead my son/daughter in the paths of righteousness for Your name's sake. My child is the head and not the tail. I pray that You will shed Your love abroad in his/her heart, and teach my child to delight in You.

Father, I thank You that You have given your angels charge over my child to lift him/her up.

Satan, I bind you and break your power over my child. You are a defeated foe. I loose the angels of God to minister to my child. I loose laborers to present Jesus Christ to my child. Holy Spirit, I ask that You draw my child to Jesus Christ and into a close, personal relationship.

Thank You, Lord, for Your gift of salvation. Thank You for saving my child. I pray these things in Jesus' name, Amen.

Scripture References

Psalm 23:3	Psalm 91:11
Deuteronomy 28:13	Matthew 9:38
Psalm 1:2	

Prayer
To Receive Salvation

Father, Your Word says that if I confess with my mouth that Jesus is Lord and believe in my heart that You raised Him from the dead, I will be saved. Lord, I confess that Jesus is Lord. I make Him Lord of my life. I believe in my heart that You raised Him from the dead.

I renounce my past life with Satan and close the door to any of his devices.

Jesus, I ask You to forgive me of my sins. Cleanse me and make me new. Thank You that old things have passed away and now all things become new, in Jesus' name. Amen.

Scripture References

John 20:31	2 Corinthians 5:17
Romans 10:9	

Prayer
for Your Child
To Come Back to the Lord

Father, my child will serve You and will not walk in the counsel of the ungodly or stand in the way of sinners, in Jesus name. He/she will be like a tree planted by the rivers of water. Whatever my child does will prosper.

Satan, I bind you and break your power over my child. I break your power to deceive my child with the world and what it offers. Devil, you loose my child, in the name of Jesus.

Jesus, I ask that You reveal Your love and mercy to my child. Take the scales off his/her eyes. Let _____ see, like the Prodigal Son did, the true condition that he/she is in. Reveal to my child that You will accept him/her back. Father, I confess that my child is coming back to Jesus, just like the Prodigal Son came back home.

Thank You, Father, for performing Your Word over my child. Thank You for bringing my child back to You. In Jesus' name, I pray these things, believing by faith that they will come to pass. Amen.

Scripture References

Psalm 1:1	Isaiah 30:18
Psalm 1:3	Acts 9:18
Matthew 16:19	Luke 15:17,18

To contact
Norvel Hayes
or
Zona Hayes Cornelison,
write them
at the address below:

P. O. Box 1379
Cleveland, Tennessee 37311

*Please include your prayer requests
and comments when you write.*

**Additional copies of this book
are available from your local bookstore,
or by writing:**

Harrison House
P. O. Box 35035 • Tulsa, Oklahoma 74153

The Harrison House Vision

Proclaiming the truth and the power
Of the Gospel of Jesus Christ
With excellence;

Challenging Christians to
Live victoriously,
Grow spiritually,
Know God intimately.

Made in the USA
Middletown, DE
29 August 2022

72598139R00038